The Community of We

Copyright © 2017 by Ernest T. Davis II. All rights reserved.

No part of this publication may be reproduced, stored in a retrieval system or transmitted in any way by means, electronic, mechanical, photocopy, recording or otherwise with the prior permission of the author except as provided by USA copyright law.

This book is designed to provide accurate and authoritative information with regard to the subject matter covered.

Published by Ernest T. Davis II

Book design copyright © 2017 by Ernest T. Davis II

ISBN: 978-0-9964988-2-1

ISBN: 978-0-9964988-3-8 (Electronic)

Religious/Christian Life

July 25, 2017

THE COMMUNITY OF WE

And they, continuing daily with one accord in the temple, and breaking bread from house to house, did eat their meat with gladness and singleness of heart, praising God, and having favour with all the people. And the Lord added to the church daily such as should be saved.

(Acts 2:46, 47 KJV)

Dedication

It is with honor and awe that I dedicate this book to Pastor Ethel Williams. She is continuing in the legacy of her husband, the late Apostle Leon Williams. I am blessed to see the result of being "The Community of We" as a foundation to reach the lost.

ACKNOWLEDGEMENT

FOREWORDS

INTRODUCTION

Chapter 1	And They Are?
Chapter 2	Daily Unity
Chapter 3	Coming Over for Dinner
Chapter 4	Covenant of a Meal
Chapter 5	Asinine Assumption of Perception
Chapter 6	Praise Is the Mortar for Lively Stones
Chapter 7	They Live With Us and Not Without Us
Chapter 8	Let God Add to the Church (Programs vs. Process)

Chapter 9	Dehumanization of a Culture is Not of God
Chapter 10	Conclusion

ACKNOWLEDGEMENT

I foremost thank God Almighty for not allowing me to choose my path of existence in this earth. Even though some paths would be more logical and even easier, we do not serve a logical God. If He were logical, I would not be breathing. Since He is illogical to the mind of man, we have untold mercy and constant grace.

I give honor to Lady Davis who is a constant example of His love to and toward me. There are times when those closest to us embrace the ministry of righteous abrasion in order to sharpen and smooth us. I welcome it while not often celebrating it during the presentation of such abrasion.

There are too many people who have imparted into my life especially with the penning of this muse. Many have challenged my belief system and doctrinal stance concerning the Christian faith which has produced a much deeper conviction in my community involvement with commitment. Our faith is not segregated and exclusive. If we have nothing in common with those not practicing the faith of the Bible, we are at least human.

I acknowledge truly the leadership of Crossroad Community Church under the vision of Pastor Anthony Wallace and his lovely wife, Pastor Margo Wallace. There are times when God will assign you to a person with no previous connection. Yet, it is ultimately for your development and to receive impartation. Just do what God says. He handles the rest in all ways.

FOREWORDS

It was December 2014 when I received a call in my office from Dr. Ernest T. Davis. At that time, I was the Director of Young People's Ministry for my former denomination. In the afternoon of the upcoming annual youth rally in Ocean City Maryland we were opening up a concert to the public. Headlining that concert was Israel Houghton and the New Breed. Dr. Davis asked about the cost and if the venue was wheelchair accessible since he was just coming through surgery which required him to be wheelchair bound. We worked out all the details and I asked him to make sure that he asked for me at the concert so I could meet him and his lovely wife in person, to thank them for coming, and praise the Lord for bringing them safely into the community that gathered for this event. I thank God for that call.

Little did I know that God was working out a wonderful friendship and brotherhood behind the scenes even before I met Dr. Davis. He told me how he had been praying for me after reading what works God was using me to perform; that of reconciliation and revival. WE both realized this when WE met. Every time that WE get together (mostly over a meal at the Smyrna Diner or soon to be meal at Jazzy Jays Soul Food) WE get some kind of Holy Ghost anointing and celebrate all the amazing things that God is doing around us, through us and in SPITE of us. WE catch a glimpse of the Kingdom of God through "The Community of WE". The Christ is there with us every time WE share an email, have a conversation through text, or break bread together. I absolutely love Ernest and his passion for sharing the truth of the Gospel of Jesus Christ in many profound, prophetic, and purposeful ways. He never goes it alone but gathers a Community of WE as a reflection of that Kingdom which is here but also not yet.

I have always been a team player. Many people have actually called me a bridge builder (especially between church folk who think they got it right but continue to be the most segregated society in the world today). If I have those qualities or gifts it is only through the grace of Jesus Christ and the power of the Holy Ghost. Maybe this is why Ernest and I were drawn to each other, so that we may be an example to the community around us that it is not about individual accomplishments. But, despite our individuality WE are called to be so much more. I have read Dr. Davis' book "The Community of We" in its entirety and several times I had to clear my eyes from the swelling of tears because these words express the passion that is on my heart for the Church to be the Bride that Christ's calls it to be… *"The Community of We"*.

May the Spirit of the Living God fall afresh on all of us as we read these words, that WE think less of ourselves and more about Christ in the community around us.

Pastor Scot Mc Clymont
4 The World Ministries
Smyrna-Clayton, DE USA

****

Every generation needs a compelling voice and a unique perspective to help clarify what God seeks to accomplish during the lifespan of that generation.

In Jesus High Priestly prayer, in the place of Gethsemane, He pleads His desire to the Father that His followers would arrive at a place of complete unity. Unity is often talked about as a lofty ideal or a practical goal, but in reality is never experienced by the larger community of believers in Christ. We agree on our faith in Jesus while disagreeing on the various and sundry points of doctrine and polity, effectively majoring in the minors. Thus we become combatants rather than co-laborers. We compete rather than compliment.

In *"The Community of We"*, Dr. Ernest Davis prosecutes the case that we must recognize our differences while appreciating that it is those very differences that provide for the proper service of the community into which God has summoned us.

Having read its entire content, I will tell you that you are about to embark on a journey. It's a journey through God's mind about how He intends to reach multiplied millions in the waning days of this dispensation. While it may seem to be an easy read, I can assure it is not a quick read. You will stop and start. Read and re-read. Contemplate, meditate and pray. While you may not be re-assigned, I am confident you will be re-calibrated. And, you will likely have a different attitude about the same aspiration.

In a world that lifts up individual accomplishment and singular identity, thank God for a prophetic view of how God sees us…and how He wants us to be.

It can no longer be about you or me. Rather, let God be glorified in The Community of We.

Pastor Anthony Wallace
Crossroad Christian Church
Dover, Delaware USA

INTRODUCTION

Recently during meditation, I asked God to show me what was before Moses was inspired to write the Book of Genesis. For weeks all I kept hearing was "*In the beginning God*". So this voice gently speaking to me caused me to really go into study concerning this. What I discovered was that the English word for God used in translations was in fact *Elohim*. This was a plural yet singular word.

I continued meditation and prayer and could see that before the foundation of the world the Lamb was slain. For quite some time I have kept that thought before me. This concept of answer being provided before there was a problem is foreign to the understanding of man and defying all human logic.

In previous works I have stated that God was not truly angry with Adam as many tried to make us think in order to scare us into a doctrine and culture of religious fear. Before the foundation of the world Adam already had provision for his fall although he didn't realize it.

When God asked what he had done, an answer would have yielded something that was also in the heavens. If the answer had been given, then God would have forgiven him for his rebellion. Paul penned in the future which was also the present at that moment of confession of our sin and God's faithfulness to forgive us; cleansing us from all unrighteousness. Yet, Adam didn't know this yet.

I am sure there will be those that may wish to attack for the purpose of debunking this muse. And, that is fine. It is a person's prerogative to do such. But, in the Hebrew language only two tenses are present. They are past, and then present with the future is combined. This lends to some of the small oddities such as when Jesus stated, "when the Holy Spirit 'is' come". According to the mindset, our present is also our future. Our past is just that; past.

Truly this event in existence was a period that was unique. Past, present and future were all together in one place in the Elohim. The Lamb had already been slain before the foundation of the world. God was on the scene waiting for just the confession or agreement of what He already knew concerning Adam. And, Adam had at his disposal life, even the Tree of Life. But, we had to go through it all for the completeness to be accomplished. Had he accepted the Sacrifice who knows what would have been instead of what has been?

But, we say that sin occurred first in the Garden. I beg to differ. Sin was first in the heavenlies with Lucifer and his angels. Pride and rebellion always leads the way. This is why the Lamb had to be slain before the foundation of the world. The Lamb was slain in a dimension outside of what we can fathom as time and existence in order to place the Sacrifice in what was recorded.

God does not dwell in our logic and understanding. He is beyond our thoughts and explanations, yet reachable through prayer. I have posed questions to many which can either cause healthy dialogue or heated debate concerning doctrinal sacred cows. One such question that was posed to a group (well receiving may I add) is, "If heaven is His throne and earth is His footstool, where is His head"? Need, I give you the visual of all the conversation and dialogue that ensued? It was quite refreshing to witness so many that would acquiesce to us not fully being able to describe God. Yet, some felt the undying need to answer this according to their historical teachings of oral tradition coupled with theological training.

Another thought offered to yet another group is that we cannot say where God dwells is what we consider time. We can describe *"chronos"*; our understanding of linear time. We can describe *"kairos"*; our understanding of the opportune timing of God. We can even describe to a point eternity; an area outside of time where time is not counted. But, does God really dwell in an area that we can describe with our understanding. Does He even dwell in eternity? Or, does He dwell outside of eternity? Again, "In the beginning God" denotes (in my humble mind) an arena that we cannot fathom on this side of glory. This is an arena outside of normal description where the Lamb was slain. It is a place that we are not privy to comprehend.

Moses had to make the Tabernacle after a heavenly example. If there was something amiss in the example then there would have been sin and unholiness in the earthly Tabernacle. What was amiss was the connection and completion of the heavens and the earth. Once Christ rose and sprinkled the sacrificed blood on the mercy seat of heaven the reconnection of holiness was made. This is why Satan can no longer ask for us in order to buffet us. He can no longer approach heaven.

In the Book of Job, Satan asked to have the ability to afflict Job. He came right with the other sons of God. The writings state "and Satan was among them. In the New Testament, Jesus informed, not warned, Peter that Satan has "asked" to sift him like wheat. He was still able to ask. Yet, with the Resurrection (and the Ascension) of Christ, His blood was sprinkled on the Mercy Seat of the heavenly Tabernacle. The Book of Hebrews explains much to understand what occurred on our behalf. His shed blood is now shed on earth AND in heaven. But, the Lamb was slain before the foundation of the world. So, I ask where was that sacrifice? Perhaps, it was in the place where His head is since His feet are on earth and He sits in Heaven. And, a note to ponder is that Thomas didn't have blood on his hands from placing them in the wounds of Jesus. Selah.

Three dimensions of the earthly Tabernacle reflect three dimensions of the heavenly Tabernacle; the Outer Court, Inner Court and the Holy of Holies. In the heavenly Tabernacle the Outer Court represents all of created man. The Inner Court represents those who have accepted Christ and are being progressively transformed into His image. The Holy of Holies represent in His presence and glory; face to face with Him.

The Lamb's Blood cleansed the heavenly example to set the standard for the earthly one. The "community" of heaven had to be cleansed. So, before Moses wrote "in the beginning" there was a community already established; God.

We were in God, and He consumed every aspect of us. We were the community of "We". We only knew God and His unspeakable love and wonder. There was no other knowledge at all. We knew nothing other than Him; *Elohim*. Before the earth, man lived in community; in unison with Him. On earth, it was God that said it is not good that man should be alone. He made for us the beginning of community out of the man on the earth; *ahdam* which included *isha* (man) and *isha* (wombed man). He made male and female just as He created in

Genesis Chapter 1. He began community on earth as it was in heaven. Out of man He made woman to continue in the perpetuation of community just as it is in heaven where we were already "created". It is on earth where He "made" us and formed us. It is here where He formed us outside of the Garden of Eden to place us in the Garden. Here is where He breathed His breath or essence in us and this body became a "living soul". We became an extension of His community.

Yet, we allowed the enemy that was cast out of the heavenly community to deceive us. In that moment our eyes were opened. What were they open to? They were opened to those things outside of the vast experienced wonderfulness of God. We began to see good and evil where previously we only viewed and experienced perfection in the presence of God. We began to view the rebellion, the war, the eviction and the transformation of the heavenly war. We saw a naked body; something we gave no thought to. And, we were afraid; something we never experienced. We lost our community that was of God; the community of "We".

Yet through the death, burial and resurrection of Christ, we regained that community even in a less than perfect environment of earth. We walk in two realms; heavenly and earthly. And, as we are on earth, we perpetuate the community of "We".

Old Timers, Baby Boomers, Generation X, Millennials and every generation coming through time, we all have a community that we must dwell in and extend outward. These people dwelling with like mind can be attributed to God's allowance for us to connect. Across racial lines there are those who will hold fast to more similarities than differences, yet recognizing the differences and even celebrate them. What are we to do? We are to live in community that may or may not involve harmony. We do have that capability within to dictate the outcome.

I often say that to state that one is Christian now is but a fad with identification to a philosophy. But, for one to be a true developing Christian there must be a developing discipleship; a disciplined growth and maturity. Therefore, we must begin to form a community that is not exclusive to just those of like minds. This is not an all-inclusive instruction on living in a community. It is not. But, in this realm, we provide for our community to grow through us thereby expanding it. And, now, let's move into our Community of We…

1

AND THEY ARE?

As I read in the passage that is the foundation of this writing, there is the initial identification of a group of people; they. In keeping with basic English written communication, they are considered to be the focus of the thought; the subject. So, exactly who are "they"?

They are the early believers who were Jewish; these who were the initial *ecclesia* or called out ones. These are people that heard the message preached by this boisterous fisherman and connected with the message through the power of the Holy Ghost. They took action! They identified. They became the people labeled as "they".

There was a religious and ceremonial foundation already laid through Judaism among the early church. "They" were already functioning within a set of religious actions that they were familiar with just as the apostles. They were Jews; practicing Jews.

> ***"And they, continuing daily with one accord in the temple, and breaking bread from house to house, did eat their meat with gladness and singleness of heart". (Acts 2:47)***

They were together and had a consistent practice concerning worship and fellowship. These people were on one accord; of one mind. This is a wonderful picture of unity without exclusiveness in this complete passage. Somehow in the process of time, we have allowed other additions to detract from the simplicity of the early church. The unity was present in the synagogue and temple as well as outside in the community among believers. I would even dare to imagine there was unity among those in the community in concert with the new believers. I am not saying that they all worshipped as one. But, I am deducting that the unity of the community was a byproduct of their belief system in the "Way".

Apostle Nate Holcomb of the Christian House of Prayer in Killeen, Texas stated so emphatically, "The church at its birth is the church at its best". There is no way possible for this statement to be untrue. The creation of man as recorded in Genesis represented us at our best. As with many things, as time progresses things creep in that often destroy the perfection of the creation under God. The same is true with the birth of what is now Christianity. It is fashionable and socially acceptable or even required for someone to identify with a belief system. However, just because one identifies with the system of stated belief does not make them a disciple. The same holds true for Christianity in this present day.

One may ascribe to the tenants of Christian ideology, yet not be a disciple who invokes discipline and growth. The youthfulness of the early church was so pure until divisions were developed, now commonly referred to as denominations or sects. There was just a willingness to love God through worship and fellowship; *koinonia.*

There are so many different ways to keep division perpetuated in the earth.

So often we wish to impose our sacred rites and desires to worship on those around us. We unknowingly and sometimes intentionally establish separation in the community, even within the community of believers. At one time it was a racial separation. Then we began cultural ones with the immigration of various ethnic groups. Now, it can appear racial, religious, cultural, doctrinal or even economical. There are so many different ways to keep division perpetuated in the earth. I am sure the enemy is thrilled at what we as the people of God do just by our zeal to be "right" without having a concern for righteousness. In order for us to be right, someone or something has to remain wrong. Therefore, if we are more concerned with being right, then we are consumed with keeping someone or a group as the wrong party. Yet, if we are concerned with being righteous, we will turn our desire over to the Lord. He is righteous, not us. And, He has already said our righteousness is no more than filthy rags. In order for us to be righteous, we must assume the position of being perpetually wrong without Him.

Whenever there is an identified subculture in the dominant culture, there will always be those who practice silent observation.

In our desire of preservation we destroy so many other things that are beneficial to the existence of the community and even the spreading of the Gospel. Jesus instructed the disciples NOT to go to anyone but to the lost sheep of Israel initially. Why? It was because Israel had to first reject Him in order for Him to go to the Gentiles that we may be grafted in. I pictured it as Israel holding all the content of grace and salvation in. They were the container. Once they rejected the content held within them, Jesus, then He was poured out for all!

The "they" of the verse were known to be apart from the general population which included other Jews and Gentiles by their worship, love and fellowship within their common community. Whenever there is an identified subculture in the dominant culture, there will always be those who practice silent observation.

We are not capable of loving in the true sense of agape.

Recently, I accepted a position of employment that many felt was beneath my qualifications and education. Yet, under the guidance of the Holy Spirit, I applied and was hired. During my brief tenure there I had constant fellowship with Him. Daily, I would quietly in my spirit listen and ask questions while performing my duties.

It was physically painful. In the previous ten to fifteen years I had suffered many physical ailments stemming from military choices, medication prescriptions and bad health choices. I had been restricted to a wheelchair at one point, on canes and crutches and even bedridden after certain surgeries. Now, I was standing on my feet for extended hours at a time. My mind was joyful at the progression, but my body reminded me that I needed to slow down.

Yet in all of this, I could pray for people coming through my station, speaking encouragement to many and even bolstering the functional faith of others. Functional faith is not just vocal acknowledgment. It is faith that doesn't need words. It is action. *Agape* is an action word as well. And, as you function in the action of *agape* the faith and unction of others begin to increase to effect changes whether large or small. But, change will occur.

So many have changed their way of thinking and began walking in a love never before witnessed!

We are not capable of loving in the true sense of *agape*. Only through the presence and power of the Holy Spirit living within us are we able to love in this manner. As a matter of fact, *agape* is only attributed to God or to us through God. It is something for us to ponder. Are we speaking *agape*? Or are we being *agape*?

Whenever there is a spiritual change or shifting one of the main dangers is creating an "us against them" environment.

I often attempt placing myself in the environment being recorded by the media to get the complete feel of what has happened. The media outlet of that day, mouth to mouth news, had already spread the event of the resurrection of this crucified and buried man, Jesus. "Everyone" knows these people have grown in number beginning with the Feast of Pentecost. So many have changed their way of thinking and began walking in a love never before witnessed! Just who are these people and why has all of this come to pass? It must have something to do with the man Jesus who "they said" arose from the dead. Besides, too many have reported that He was walking on the earth and talking to people. Too many eye witnesses have forsaken all to tell this truth at all costs! Surely, it required the attention of even the skeptics.

Sadly, "church people" often set up walls to the surrounding community while misquoting selected excerpts of the Bible to support some form of separation.

Whenever there is a spiritual change or shifting one of the main dangers is creating an "us against them" environment. Many will undoubtedly get the former statement and shut down. But, I assure you that this happens on both sides of the equation. Ones that name the name of Christ can be just as guilty causing the other side to shut down to anything we have to say concerning the One that is the Source of life and change. Yet, we as Disciples of Christ need to ensure this does not happen. I am in no way saying that we are to accept, condone or participate in behaviors or lifestyles apart from what brings God glory. But, we are not to demonize anyone that is not in our lifestyle to the fact of beating them down. This is where *agape* is lived.

I have witnessed a gentleman that really attempted to insert his own form of righteousness into someone else's life. He was wrong; period. While there is the law of God, there is also the law of the land. He was a busybody into someone else's household.

A couple had been cohabitating for quite some time together. As with all couples married, single or whatever differences arose. He became the 'listening ear and soft shoulder' for all women who had trouble with those 'sinful men'. In this one situation he attempted to impose 'the law of God' in a situation where the person did not want to leave. Jesus never forced anyone to leave anything. They willingly followed.

"Zeal without wisdom will kill you."

In his self-righteous actions, he was straddling the fence; transgressing the law of the land. His zeal for religious meddling could have resulted in domestic violence for all parties beginning with him and possibly extending to the woman. No amount of reason could pierce his mind to understand there are laws of privacy that must be adhered to. I kept it in prayer for his safety. While he was a self-proclaimed prophet of

God that would root out all unrighteousness any time he would find it, he lacked street smarts as we would call it in urban areas.

To make a long story short, the woman was playing him in such a way as to make her paramour jealous; ready to do bodily harm to this man. Yet he could not see it. His focus was on rescuing the damsel in distress that he created in his own mind. Therefore, there was a deeper situation that could've ensued; the need for traumatic injury treatments and possibly orthopedic treatment after consciousness was gained. I won't go into some of the other details that let me know this man was just a scared coward hiding behind a religious tirade. We must be careful not to become a self-appointed Holy Ghost police officer. My prayer was answered. He did not end up like the Sons of Sceva as mentioned in Acts 19. The woman rejected him which left him humiliated and eventually moving away. It could have ended up very badly. An early saying that I would give as a point of instruction to early mentees is, "Zeal with wisdom will kill you".

We must remember two things. The primary thing is that sin is not a degree or progressive thing. Sin equals death, period. There is no big sin vs. a little sin. And, next, we were also in sin apart from accepting Christ. So regardless of how good we thought our lifestyle or actions were, we were also living ungodly. Apart from Christ is death. This is very simple.

"…we don't live in a Christian world."

Sadly, "church people" often set up walls to the surrounding community while misquoting selected excerpts of the Bible to support some form of separation. Again, I am not saying to be participants in all of the deviant living witnessed by the world. But, how will we share the Gospel in love if we charge out of our doors only at certain times and practically beat someone in the head with a Bible then retreat back behind barriers immediately? We can't. If that mentality was true then when Jesus walked the earth for His ministry the whole earth would have been saved before He ascended. We must walk as He did; among the people and not apart from them as the Pharisees.

I watched a young woman mature and matriculate to college and beyond to medical school. She gave me a powerful answer. I asked why, with such pressure from others, she chose the college she attended. I was floored at her answer. She said she didn't choose a Christian college because we don't live in a Christian world. And, she is so very correct! I have watched her in society as a missionary of sorts; living a life in Christ while not alienating others.

Our "us against them" posture should be only to be determined to show *agape* love toward those who are not "like" us. This was the case with the early church. They were known for their steadfastness in the temple and fellowship in the community. One will be surprised how this is observed.

… we cannot share the Gospel though our bullet proof glass of separation while we remain "protected".

When I was young, I had the chance to witness many religious movements. One group in particular surely was steadfast in their temple gathering. They were also in the community constantly going from house to house amongst themselves. The only time they went house to house concerning anyone else or mingled with those without their belief was to proselytize the people. Even in attending funerals, they would not come depending on how the life celebration was being conducted and the location. This was even true of immediate family. When I asked one person why this was so, they responded curtly referring me specific Biblical passages. But, as a young person unpolluted by many religious and even social ills, there is an inward sparkle of God speaking to things that are not right. I say this because we cannot share the Gospel though our bullet proof glass of separation while we remain "protected". We must be among the people. We must be as Christ; touching those without our own established religious circles and quirks. Let us remove the "us against them" mentality. Selah.

2

DAILY UNITY

Within the pericope of Scripture a daily occurrence of unity is noted. As we grow in Christ so should our desire and need to be unified on a continual basis within all aspects of life. This should not be something that only occurs when problematic situations arise sometimes caused by our own actions. It must be a daily life blood of our existence. Unity begins with the individual extending to those around him, whether it is family or community. Unity is then connected as we accept Christ as Savior in order for Him to now become Lord. God is in Unity with Himself. He is Unity manifested. We are to be in unity with one another as we are in Him. It is the only way where we begin to be the "Community of We".

Unity is never a singular concept involving only you. Unity must be "we", never "I". Our Constitution of the United States never began as "I the Person". It begins as "We the People". Somehow in the last two millenniums we have grown into a false Lone Ranger Christianity that is as effective as a screen door on a submerged submarine. It begins with thinking that we are exclusive to a group that embraces a certain belief. Then if we are not physically present in that group there is a mindset that we are an island amongst our own self. Nothing could be so further from the truth.

Unforgiveness is the catalyst for disunity.

Mankind always has something in common with another man; God. Whether that person believes in God or not there must be some form of unity on this earth if nothing else but to procreate for the human race. While I choose not to force my faith on others, I do share my faith in ways that make no mistake that I know my God is sovereign. How do I do this? I love with all my power in the *agape* love that only God can give me. This is not the love of going to Him when wronged or mistreated for Him to kill the offender in retribution. Why? Because, He gently reminds me of what was forgiven for me. Once that is presented, I must move away and stop being so adamant about how much wrong I endured and realize how much wrong I have done either intentionally or unintentionally. Unforgiveness is the catalyst for disunity. I am not saying that one that forgives must immediately restore all trust. But, I am stating emphatically that forgiveness is immediate while trust and the rebuilding of unity is a time of rebuilding.

Unity is destroyed by offense. I once heard a quote from a friend that communication destroys all confusion. While the quote is true, it must be supplemented. Mutual communication destroys all confusion. I would say that the vast amount of offense that has occurred in my life has been due to a lack of communication; even wrong perception of the communication. This occurs in the Christian community as well. Our lack of communication begins with a soulish or humanistic interpretation of the word of God.

Our biggest enemy is disunity.

There are so many different views and doctrines within Christianity until it will discourage even a seasoned theologian if allowed to stand. Yet, the most powerful and knowledgeable teacher that one can sit under is the Holy Spirit. He is the One sent from God to guide, teach and correct us! God the Father made the plan. God the Son carried it out. And, God the Holy Spirit enables us to live the carried out plan!

Our biggest enemy is disunity. Unity should be our greatest desire; the desire to be a part of something. And, the culmination of this is to become one just as Jesus and the Father are One. It is this innate desire to belong to something that drives us to join "groups" for identification, function, protection and fulfillment. The initial group that we are part of should be family at birth.

It is terrible to see a newborn shunned at birth. Something within this precious being screams for protection, acceptance and nurturing. Yet, there are those who will abandon one. While surrogate and adoptive families fill the immediate void once that child discovers that they are not the biological offspring of those surrogate parents and family that void of rejection and abandonment is torn open. I have met adopted children that had no idea they were adopted until adulthood, yet there was this innate inkling that something was amiss.

Once they discovered that they were adopted an instinct rose up in them to find their "family" at all costs. Some even became bitter while at the same time needing to "look them in the face" to find out why they were placed in the situation. The very same thing can be experienced by those who were raised by a grandparent knowing fully who their biological parent or parents are. It's that need to be in union; unity with a group.

The image of God needs the image of God to be the image of God.

Our early church fathers knew and embraced this concept. They knew that not only was their existence in the community enveloped in unity, their development in Christ was in unity with Him primarily and others in Him secondarily. Today with our mentality of "it's all about me", we seem to have lost that truth. We are made in the image and likeness of God. When that knowledge was given in the first chapter of Genesis, no mention was made of our religious affiliation, church denomination or even ethnic group. We are made in the image of God; period. Therefore with the adage of birds of a feather flock together, we must make our own adage. The image of God needs the image of God to be the image of God. It is just that simple. We are His image. Therefore, we cannot look at another and say that is not His image. All people on this earth are His image and His likeness. We are the one trying to cover the image and destroy the intended unity given us before the foundation of the world.

We are to be a walking example of community.

Have we ever given serious thought about from whence we came? We came from the Ultimate Unity Example that cannot be fathomed or humanly explained! I am always in a state of awe at the first four words in the Bible; Genesis 1:1 "In the beginning God". A Hebrew translation would tell us the in the beginning "*Elohim*".

Elohim is a pluralistic yet singular identity of God. So the initial earthly "peek" of our wonderful God is that He is community and unity! He is three Persons yet one Person. And, here we are the image of Him. We are to be a walking example of community. We were in Him prior to being dispatched and released into this physical realm we call earth. Therefore, we pre-existed as a community in the community of Elohim. How is it that we want to alter our primary spiritual existence in this physical world? We can't. Even a hermit will come into contact with another physical and living being even if it is an animal. Yet, we attempt vainly to not live in any form of community. It is truly vain to try.

3

COMING OVER FOR DINNER

There are times when things in the Bible can be so cut and dried. Yet, there are times when the words will cut, but we never dry. Such is the thought of "breaking bread from house to house".

While it is understood that the saints were a community within a community, I am in awe at what they lived among this culture. Selling all things so that everyone had everything in common would be a frowned upon concept today. Yet, it was needed for the early church to thrive initially. Another musing would be the breaking of bread from house to house.

I currently reside in a community classified as a residential development. This is a collection of like dwellings often built on a specific tract of land. Often there is an elected governmental body that ensures all bylaws and deed restrictions remain. There is no individuality as to where we just do as we wish. Our neighbors and the body must be addressed.

... the early saints had no agenda other than to strengthen unity.

In this community there are many people of different backgrounds, cultures and religion. Yet, there are times when there is a community function that causes us to come together to eat. This doesn't give me the example of the early Church. Why? It is because it is not a daily occurrence. It may be an annual occurrence, but not daily. We have to have a reason for this annual meal whether for business or just to meet one another. But, the early saints had no agenda other than to strengthen unity. I would even dare say that others outside their belief system were also welcomed.

A meal in early biblical history was considered an act of friendship and covenant. Since the first disciples were Jewish, this was an important tenant of being within a community. Feasts, covenants and even treaties were held over meals. The example of remembering the Lord Jesus Christ was held over a meal. So, eating or sustenance is a very integral part of being a community.

One of the sacraments of our faith is communion; common union. This sacrament is often performed only once a month in many congregations with a ritualistic flair. Yet, the Book of Acts never limits this to once a month or once a day for that matter. Could it be that the distinction in Acts 2:46 is that they were going from house to house for communion as well as a meal? Could they have had two scenarios of eating; breaking bread and the meal eaten with gladness? I hope to challenge the reader to give this thought and prayer for revelation. There are things written in our Canon that cannot be cut and dried. They must be pored over with while allowing the Holy Spirit to teach us.

When one attends a meal or barbeque with others, there is a degree of openness.

It is my personal belief that the meal eaten with gladness was a community one; the meal of the Community of We. In this meal, barriers were down because of the meal. When one attends a meal or barbeque with others, there is a degree of openness. One normally doesn't come to the meal with all barriers totally up. Otherwise, you would never eat! There is something about breaking bread with another. There must be a level of trust if in nothing else but their ability to satisfy a human need; hunger.

Any other example could have been used by Christ to remember Him. Yet, He chose a meal; a simple meal. In many instances of a family reunion a meal is the drawing factor. Those who may not come for any other activity will attend the meal. So many instances of a meal are mentioned biblically until we must acknowledge the importance of it in community. Psalm 23:5 denotes the preparation of a meal in community with even enemies present. I don't mean for all to agree with me, but that is a perfect example of a family reunion. The meal is prepared in the middle of a society that may not be friendly. It is the meal that will draw one to another.

I once lived in an area of urban unrest. There was a restaurant owner who prepared the best fried chicken I have ever tasted; and I have sampled a lot. But, he was right in the middle of a gang ridden area. People were drawn from all over. As a matter of fact when visiting the area that is one of my mandated stops. I remember one of my many visits there, a woman from well outside the city came in to pick up an order that had been placed. During her few minutes while in the establishment some activity outside startled her. She asked me if I would escort her to her car. There was no threat to her. But, her perception was that of danger. I agreed and escorted her to her car. While walking I asked why she came so far into an area she was clearly not used to functioning in. She replied, "There is no other chicken as good as this and I wanted only this chicken". I still hold this memory today as to the lengths someone will go to for a good meal.

While the community most likely was similar in dress and culture, there was a difference spiritually.

In this mindset, a good meal will open a person up. Yet, while they are open it is up to the host or hosts what will be served to them both naturally and spiritually. Paul spoke of first the natural then the spiritual. I have visited many shelters and soup kitchens that minister to both needs either separately or simultaneously. I think we need to return to breaking bread from house to house. There is something about the conception that may very well give us a key to reaching those in our community.

There definitely must be a form of subsistence if we wish to have a community with all people. The Community of We must form with meals involved, both natural and spiritual. While the community most likely was similar in dress and culture, there was a difference spiritually.

A point of focus is that there is no mention of anyone placing requirements on those eating or coming to eat that would make them pre-qualify for the meal. No assumption was made that the individuals sharing the meal had to prequalify or measure up to a standard. In our present religious circles we are often subconsciously made to measure up to another's preconceived notions. While I am sure there are rules for basic behavior, there can be no prequalification and expectation for many that are coming to the Lord. He didn't have it for us. The Community of We only served the meal. And, that meal involved the Bread of Life. Selah.

4

COVENANT OF A MEAL

I have discovered that a meal is something that brings people together. It is a meal that causes peace to abound even in the midst of turmoil. When one sits down to have a meal with another, it is a sign of trust; of covenant.

There is a peaceful magic about barbeque and music.

I recall reading military accounts of World War II where soldiers on each side of the conflict came together for a Christmas meal even in combat. The meal united them as brothers. Even in my own military experience when there were intermural conflicts, often a good meal solved differences even to the point of forming friendships. There is a peaceful magic about barbeque and music.

Agreements have been made over meals. In the various governments of the world, banquets are prepared for visiting dignitaries. When a powerful dignitary comes to a country, the banquet is exquisite. No cost is spared on the sumptuous delicacies that are presented. Even in cases of what is considered by many as base living, a meal is what unites people.

There are no boundaries or prejudices with hunger.

In the community, there is no difference in this unspoken rule. I have observed many instances where a church may sell dinners or host some type of barbeque. People form lines to have a taste of fried fish, soul food, fried chicken or even just spaghetti. It is the meal that attracts people.

In an area that I resided, church meals were valued as a treasure by all. Regardless of one's spiritual state, if a certain church advertised meals all would come. And, even within the operation of "selling dinners" there were personal "cooks" that were celebrities in the community. What I did notice was that anyone with any issue could get a meal and often get prayer while waiting for it. It was a community effort to prepare the food, market and distribute the food. In turn, the people would come to the food which allowed for a fellowship even if it was only for a short period of time.

There are no boundaries or prejudices with hunger. If a person is experiencing dire hunger, they could care less who would supply this need. I have witnessed many with religious dietary laws break those laws because of hunger. Not all may do this. But, in my own observation many do. I do not judge them in any fashion. I have broken my own self-imposed dietary restrictions because of hunger. I have dined on dishes that I swore I would not touch with a ten foot pole. And, in retrospect with the hunger that was upon me, it was good! Will I try it again? Only if that hunger prevails to the level of abandonment.

While Adam allowed his blood to be tainted by food, Christ remained pure.

In the Garden of Eden, it was food that was used to tempt man; drawing him into rebellion and condemnation. Nothing else was presented to him. It was fruit; plain and simple. A covenant was made with blood in that act of rebellion. And, it would take blood to undo it; the Blood of the Lamb. While Adam allowed his blood to be tainted by food, Christ remained pure. The enemy tempted Jesus at a point of pure hunger with food. Yet, He did not succumb to the temptation. I am glad that my Savior didn't sell me out for a couple of loaves of bread. Hunger is a powerful weapon!

I would like to veer slightly only to return from the subject of covenant. Adam allowed his blood to become contaminated because of his desire to eat the forbidden fruit. Was there a hunger? Perhaps there was not a physical one, but a hunger nonetheless. Therefore, God could not allow him to provide the seed of redemption. It was given to Eve that her Seed would be the one. In Genesis 3:15, the seed of Adam was not mentioned. It was only the "Seed" of Eve.

Is it so uncanny that a meal or morsel caused the fall?

When a man impregnates a woman, it is his seed that grows in her. While that seed receives nutrients from the mother's blood, their blood never mixes. It is the blood of the seed provider that is in the child. Therefore, Adam or any of his descendants could not provide the seed for redemption. Only God could provide the perfect and holy

Seed which was Jesus. Yet, He had to enter this world according to what was established; a woman's womb. No earthly man could father such a child. God provided the Seed. And, that Seed never had the blood of fallen man. But, for nine months He shared the meal of man through woman or wombed man. I marvel at the complex simplicity that the Lord created man with.

I return now to covenant. Is it so uncanny that a meal or morsel caused the fall? I think not. God also provided for a meal in the covenant of Passover which foreshadowed the meal to come. What is considered as the Last Supper was a covenant given to us to remember the promises of God and the upcoming sacrifice of Christ. God uses meals to form covenants. Throughout the Old and New Testaments meals were spoken of as signs of covenants and honor. It is no wonder God has used this as a form of establishing community.

During the meal one is taking something external and making it internal. It is likened as having another source of life enters into your own body to provide or sustain life. This is a form of covenant; allowing an external to bond with your internal.

I cannot break bread with someone that I am at odds with.

In communities, meals are often considered gathering places. In the Scriptural reference, they went from house to house breaking break; covenant meals. This brings people closer. I cannot break bread with someone that I am at odds with. Personally for me that just does not happen. In order for me to share a meal with a person, there must be some form of agreement possibly even birthed out of need. But, I must have some sort of agreement even if it is to curb hunger; covenant.

This is how we function in our community. We have a need to share food at times. Only in certain religious communities has there been a total segregation of meals. Some very orthodox religions will only eat foods prepared a certain way. Yet, they still may purchase and consume other goods not readily provided in their beliefs. There is still another crossing of beliefs concerning foods.

Houses of faith for many religions use this human need to bring others close to them. Dinners, cookouts and the like are used to bring people into their culture or hear their message. Passover Seders have become very popular in Christian circles because of the Hebraic roots of Christianity. Church feasts of all types have been used as evangelistic tools. People that engage in feeding those others that are less fortunate engage in forming covenants with them; covenants of assistance. So, when we prepare and share a meal, we form covenants.

This is exactly what the early church did. While it may not be clear if they did it only within their own circles or with everyone in the community, they formed daily covenants. They went from house to house breaking bread. However they went about this business, the community was taking notice. And, when you feed people, others are watching not only what you feed them but how you feed them. More than just the obvious covenant is being formed.

5

ASSININE ASSUMPTION OF PERCEPTION

A struggle in naming this chapter ensued once I realized a certain topic would have to be addressed. People of God can have a tendency to assume those that are not "part of this movement" have no worth and are subconsciously deemed heathen. This is very far from truth.

There are many cultures that have been around prior to Christianity, or are just different in expression of their culture. Often, those who are self-proclaimed sociological missionaries tend to view all of humanity and community through their eyes. Assumptions are made concerning living arrangements.

This was a grave error in European colonialism. While they truly believed they had a superior culture, in fact it was not. It was different, but not superior. Today, we still witness the damage that has occurred with that misconception. Aborigines, Native Americans, Africans, Taino Indians of the Caribbean; they have all suffered from colonialism's assumption.

One of the oldest civilizations in the world and even mentioned in the Bible is Ethiopia. Many would consider Ethiopia an African nation. In fact, it was considered a continent; the Land of Burnt Face. We find it mentioned in Exodus. But, there is a veiled reference of it in Genesis as well. This designation covered all of what is considered the present day African continent. One would do well to research the history of Africanus a well-known Roman general and Hannibal. I enjoy dropping nuggets of curiosity throughout a musing to engage those who wish to grow in understanding.

This same mentality has perpetuated itself into today's Christian mindset. There are so many false assumptions concerning humanity until it is dangerous to not study the Word of God. If we are not sensitive to the leading of the Holy Spirit we will believe the lie of the enemy and attempt to make everyone into our own little society. Could it be that your society is in error and needing correction?

Christianity is following of the tenants of Christ. It has nothing to do with being a disciple of Christ.

We need to be very careful of what we assume especially when it comes to our faith and growth. I continually remind the readers of a fact. Christianity is following of the tenants of Christ. It has nothing to do with being a disciple of Christ. One can identify as a Christian and not be a disciple as many vocalize in this day and age. Many self-identify as Christian for various reasons. I would wager that many of those who self-identify as Christian may not be disciples which live a lifestyle of spiritual growth and development in His teachings.

There is a present mindset that if a person lives in a manufactured home, there must be poverty.

Recently, an assumption was made in my community concerning a neighboring community's living arrangements. There is a present mindset that if a person lives in a manufactured home, there must be poverty. Such madness can be deceiving unless we take time to get to know those of the community. With the various housing scenarios today, many choose living arrangements that are not the norm compared to yesteryear's norm. Such was the case with this community.

While many may in fact live in such an arrangement for reasons assumed, not all do. It can be a convenience for those not desiring some of the responsibilities that would accompany another form of residence. In essence, many may choose to rent instead of purchase. Many may be akin to living in manufactured housing compared to construction. Rural development has taken a turn from urban dwelling. Suburban development can be just a "dash" between urban and rural. And, variations are not just limited to the stated examples. We need to understand the Community of We does not fit a cookie cutter mold. Selah.

6

PRAISE IS THE MORTAR FOR LIVELY STONES

When building a structure with stones or bricks there must be a "mortar" to keep everything in place. Since we are lively stones according the Word of God, we must have something to keep us in place. There must be a mortar between us as individual stones. That mortar is praising God.

I am taken back so often that it may seem as if I am just out of this world. And, I am.

When people of God come together there is what is referred to as praise reports among them. Praise and worship are two different actions. Praise is telling others what God has done. Worship is telling Him who He is. Everyone can praise God. But, everyone cannot worship Him. There are times when I am worshipping in His presence. I don't need to tell Him what He has done. He knows and hasn't forgotten. And, often I can't name all that He has done because other instances constantly come up! So, I just tell Him who He is to me. And, even then I am operating on limited revelation. He is ever-evolving in who He is to me. Yet, when I praise Him, I am telling others what He has done for me. I give them details. I am taken back so often that it may seem as if I am just out of this world. And, I am. I can't find the words at times to even describe how His actions have affected me. This is when tears of indescribable joy just flow. I once penned the term "maniacal praise" to describe a dimension of praise (not just going crazy in physical action and movement) where my spirit is within leaping while being overwhelmed in His presence.

I have many instances in my life. Even from my youth in retrospect, I see His hand on me and my existence in all things. From my very first encounter with Him, things were put in motion for me to praise Him continuously. Therefore, I am full of praise when I come in contact with others of like faith.

Christianese is a term I use to describe when a person punctuates almost every other word with religious jargon such as, "amen", "Father God", "hallelujah" or the likes.

There are limitations on praise to those without, however. While they may not ascribe certain events and activities to praise, they still witness these events. This is why we are living epistles to be read by all men. They read our lives often to see God written on the culture. We cannot bombard them with religious jargon and things they may not fathom. And, they need proof, not just statements. Also, they need to see that the praise report is not tainted by wasting the blessing on something questionable. In giving them a praise report, we should strive to speak the language of understanding; not "Christianese".

Christianese is a term I use to describe when a person punctuates almost every other word with religious jargon such as, "amen", "Father God", "hallelujah" or the likes. I have heard this described as vain repetitions and babblings. I tend to agree. Yet it is not my intention to castigate those to whom this was taught and required as doctrinal function. There is much more we can agree upon than focusing on this one point of disagreement. When we are speaking to those without the congregation in the community, will they understand what is trying to be communicated? I doubt it. Even in this form of communication we can dishearten them with a separate identity to another. Our praise should be immersed in standard communication, not with peppered jargon.

There was an instance where I gave praise to God while in a doctor's office for an injury. The doctor heard exactly what I was speaking of. She was Hindu and let me know as such. Never did I attack her gods. But, I did tell her about the Most High God and how it was that I was still functioning for so long with the injury.

The injury was of such a nature that she was baffled that I functioned and was even walking with assistance for an extended period of time. When I returned to schedule the painful surgery, she had researched first Jesus Christ, then my surgical procedure. She heard my praise and the Holy Spirit began drawing her in. Praise is a farmer planting the Seed. When she could not decipher any logical reason on the MRI for my mobility while not wincing in crucial pain, she went to the One that kept me mobile.

I didn't beat her over the head and tell her how wrong she was for not belonging to Christ. I simply dwelt in the present Community of We before me; planting the seed that another would water. I was told later that the "seed" that was planted caused such a dilemma in her belief system until she gravitated toward other believers in her office. In turn they also began to "water" one another in the Community of We until there began to be fruit among that microcosm of medical professionals.

I witnessed something that disturbed me not long ago. At a convenience store someone was actually laying a foundation of praise concerning the Word to an individual that was not involved with any church. As they continued talking, the individual began to draw on the testimony. The brother in Christ was speaking in a normal way, not making religious jargon his form of communication. Then another known Christian walked up.

I did not invite him to church. I repeat. I did NOT invite him to church.

He immediately switched his conversation from Standard English with a hint of urban dialogue to Christianese. The unsaved brother walked away the moment a distinction was made to Brother "Such and Such" and the individual that was not churched. This is a danger although not intentional in its occurrence.

…"I don't remember where it is, but give me five minutes".

I encountered the gentleman at a later time. I gave him the pleasantries of the day and struck up a conversation with him. I did not invite him to church. I repeat. I did NOT invite him to church. I began giving a praise report in the spoken language of how God works in my life. Many questions proceeded from his mouth. I answered all that I could answer and told him that others I would go find his answer. I don't believe that there will be many instances where all questions posed to a believer will be able to be answered. We should never be afraid to say that we must go find an answer.

An elderly woman who has since gone to be with the Lord, used to give an answer that made me smile with adoration. When she was asked where something was in the Bible. She would say, "I don't remember where it is, but give me five minutes". And she would find it. While this is not an excuse to not memorize God's word, it does ease the unrighteous expectation that one should memorize everything including the publisher's information and address.

We must speak the language of the Community of We; simple communication.

Then I asked the gentleman why he couldn't talk to others with such questions. He stated, "When I do speak to a Christian, there is an "us and them" mentality". I asked him to explain. He explained that if a Christian speaks to him all is good until another Christian walks up. Immediately at that point there becomes a separate communication to "the other" person. Evidently, this was such a turn off until he ascribed this to all Christians. I have witnessed this often. People, this should not be.

Our praise should be in such simplistic language as to everyone can understand it without us peppering it with Christianese or making distinction because Brother A or Sister B walked by. We must speak the language of the Community of We; simple communication. Our normal enthusiasm that God has and still is operating in our life should plant the initial seed of hearing followed by the next seed of observation. Either of these seed will produce the fruit of salvation as the Holy Spirit draws them to Himself.

7

THEY LIVE WITH US AND NOT WITHOUT US

I am not sure what prompted me to begin poring over this pericope of Scripture. But, I do know that we as Christians may have some things askew from what was originally intended in the Book of Acts. I recall only one time when the saints were segregated from the rest of the culture.

There are times when God will speak instructions but not in chronological order.

The disciples were given implicit instructions by Christ to go and wait in Jerusalem. Yet, this instruction came on the heels of Him telling them to go into the entire world to preach the Gospel. There are times when God will speak instructions but not in chronological order. So, in the Upper Room the disciples waited for the promised power endued from on high. This appears to be the only time they were separate from the outside culture. Yet, there was a reason for this. The outside culture was not the nucleus of the new organism (the church is an organism not an organization) that was created.

Praising God, and having favour with all the people. And, the Lord added to the church daily such as should be saved. (Acts 2:47)

The new organism had left the Upper Room. Peter preached the initial sermon of evangelism. Many came to the faith; a megachurch was birthed. And, they continued living within the community. I cannot see where they became a reclusive commune. I read that there was constant interaction with the community in this passage. While there are those who would say that they withdrew from 'those sinners'.

I would not agree. If this were so, the Lord would not add daily to the church those to be saved. If the community was already saved by accepting Christ, would they be "re-saved"?

> ***You cannot add to anything that has already been totaled.***

Believers were praising God; the mortar for all the lively stones being together. Having favor with all men would entail interaction with all men. I don't like the principle of eisegesis where something is placed into the Scripture unless there is a true picture that is painted in the surrounding verses. In this case, it is so. You cannot add to anything that has already been totaled. God cannot add to His completed action as outlined in this passage.

The favor enjoyed by the early church existed because they were among those that were not part of their original number. They were possibly those who were utilizing their option to "wait and see". This is the same today when we come to the Lord. Many that may be familiar with our past life will adopt this option. Sadly, they may also not look for anything new, but a reminder of everything old in order to be used by the accuser of brethren. This hinders if not destroys their possibility of stepping out in faith.

If there is no exposure, there is no evangelism.

I have listened to and witnessed many well-meaning saints that state they would never do business with the world. This mindset also is perpetuated with those outside of the church as well concerning those who name the name of Christ. If there is no exposure, there is no evangelism. It's just that simple. While I did state that we don't need to prove our Christian standing with quoting Bible verses as to bombard those who are without with "holiness", we are to live in their presence as not snobby people desiring to appear holy, but loving them with agape through the Holy Spirit while not condoning actions.

I have many examples that come to mind. I will only give a short accounting of two. In the first, there is a man who is an awesome cook. He witnessed transitions in my walk at least twice. I noticed one day that he was listening intently as I was speaking to another of his customers that wanted to bash Christians.

In listening to the Holy Spirit, I did not engage this man with an argumentative spirit. I only asked one question. I asked him, "If he felt all Christians were frauds and needed to find the true god of his understanding, how would he present his god to me that would show him love regardless of his actions toward me?" He blew up in anger and went through the roof. I maintained my dignity and continued waiting for my order. The man couldn't answer that.

We must be very careful not to place undue burdens of proof on those coming to the Lord.

I continued to engage him, but out of an attentive love. Eventually, he confessed that he had been hurt many times by those in churches. Evidently, many had come to proselytize him, only to place undue burdens on him to prove his conversion. It caused him so much pain until the root of bitterness took hold. We must be very careful not to place undue burdens of proof on those coming to the Lord. There is no way that a new Christian can fully understand old traditions that often hold no doctrinal or theological value. Please keep the sacred cow in the pastures of tradition and not in the doctrine of salvation.

Granted there was one time when I would have been ready to go toe to toe with him on all issues presented. But, I thank God for a constant maturing in my walk which can only occur by sitting under personal leadership; a pastor. It would have damaged him more. That man today is a pillar in the community at one of the churches there. We should be very careful what seed we plant. We will receive a harvest for it. And, we will have to give an account of our actions done in this body.

The man behind the counter was listening intently. He was preparing my food. But, one ear was pretty much the microphone between us. As, I would occasionally visit the restaurant, I noticed my orders began to get heavier and heavier. I didn't complain!

At that time I welcomed the 'favor among all men' especially this man. An extra portion surely would bless me in the form of leftovers.

I felt like Phillip encountering the Ethiopian eunuch.

One day, I popped into the restaurant during a slow time. He was sitting behind the counter reading one of the small New Testaments that the Gideons pass out. I think I startled him. He put it down to take my order. Casually, I asked him what he was reading. I felt like Phillip encountering the Ethiopian eunuch.

Our discussion lasted for the full preparation of my 'heavy' plate again. This man was known in the community as a standup guy, not allowing any intimidation from any of the gangs of the area. No graffiti ever marked his walls. No one ever got out of line on his corner. Yet, here he is asking simple questions. I was honored to be part of his answers. He made a statement that I remember to this day. He said that if I ever started a church in the area he would surely come and join to us by attending regularly. This really blew me away. I was floored and beyond humbled.

I moved from the area but return often. I always try to stop in the restaurant because his fried chicken is pure rapture. My wife accompanies me in the establishment. He blesses her with more fish on a plate than can be on display in the seafood section of a store.

... we think everyone God uses has to be in churches and making our roster for Christianity.

On one of my last visits, a man came in that I recognized. He said he was thankful for what the owner had talked to him about. Evidently it was a conversation about God and being one with Him. Imagine this! This man refuses to step foot in a church but is preaching. Wow. And, we think everyone God uses has to be in churches and making our roster for Christianity. Before I knew it my wife, myself and my brother were all testifying and praising God. (The first part of verse 47 gives us instruction.)

Word does seem to travel in urban communities quicker than in others.

I learned from the visitor that not only had he planted a church in the south, he also remembered me in a condition that I will not address here. He had 'heard' that I was now a man of God and walking with Him. Word does seem to travel in urban communities quicker than in others. I rejoiced and gave him my contact information.

As he left and we were standing there, I asked the owner did he remember his statement about me starting a church there. He said he did and got silent. I told him that I wasn't returning to start a church. But, he blessed me with that confession. His sigh of relief was deep. I guess he thought he would have to honor his words. And, he is truly a man of his word.

We can wound inside of the church.

There are many such as the people in this example that are wounded by well-meaning saints. However, in their intended actions casualties are produced. It does not have to be outside of the church exclusively. We can wound inside of the church. And, this is where much of the injury occurs. Yet, there is a difference in 'who' is wounded. Some may be able to withstand it. Some cannot. Some can withstand injury and continue on.

Others may only withstand a quick sting and fall back.

I was told by a leader that I spoke like a wounded man from the saints. With all the respect that I have for this man, I still could not just allow that to be wrongly stated. I addressed it as the Holy Spirit was giving it to me; a prophetic moment to address an ongoing problem in the fellowship.

A wounded warrior never has that option to just leave and lick his wounds.

I responded with love and sadness. I stated that yes I had been wounded in the walls, yet allowed it because of the assignment. But, there was difference between a wounded man and a wounded warrior. A wounded man leaves and chooses never to return to the site of injury.

A wounded warrior never has that option to just leave and lick his wounds. He can possibly be evacuated if the wound is life threatening and debilitating. But, he may very well be reassigned to his original unit where he was injured. I considered myself a warrior and didn't run every time a person decided to wound me whether intentionally or not. As with the military ideology, the accomplishment of the mission is of priority. This is the same with the assignment of God.

These are things we must remember in order to facilitate favor from all men being directed to us as saints. Then God can pick the fruit of our labor and plant them in the Kingdom. But, first we must display the Kingdom.

I never made any fuss of his cursing and comments.

The final example is one that keeps me smiling whenever I encounter the gentleman. We discovered an awesome mechanic that is very proficient in his field. I never made any fuss of his cursing and comments. I came to him because on our initial visit he stood by his work without even knowing us.

In the time of getting to know him the very first thing out of my mouth was not that I was a man of God and a member of a specific church. It was praise for him being proficient and giving us splendid service. Also, as I listened, I discovered that he had been wronged by a professing Christian; deeply wounded. He was very angry with that and said he wouldn't work on any other Christian's car. He was livid with everyone that came in with symbols on their car but didn't want to pay the price of repairs. I couldn't understand this since his labor prices were much lower than the competition with service above reproach. There were times that words came out of his mouth that would make a sailor cry. Yet, I remained silent until prompted to speak by the Lord.

We engaged in conversation that described church members and societal Christians compared to disciples; those striving constantly to grow.

When I did speak, I identified both my wife and I as Disciples of Christ and just not casual Christians. He was silent. We engaged in conversation that described church members and societal Christians compared to disciples; those striving constantly to grow. He said that because of us, he had to rethink his stance on all Christians. Mind you, I only planted and possibly watered. We have since formed a relationship. I approach him with the wisdom ascribed to Saint Francis of Assisi.

"Preach Christ at all times and sometimes use words."

Little by little he warmed up. And as with the restaurant owner, favor is constantly given. In turn, any place that he goes to work, I will take our vehicles. There are times when he will work for other various establishments. And we follow him there for his excellent service. It blesses him by our fellowship and friendship and also the owners with our business.

I prayed for wisdom and prophesied to him.

He got into trouble when an encounter ensued with the other Christian mentioned earlier about a bill due him well over two years. He didn't heed my advice to just write the debt off. Words were exchanged. A court case ensued with charges against my mechanic that could have landed him in jail because of his words. This whole time he was a single father and truly handling his responsibilities with a kindergartener. He confided in me the situation. As a matter of fact I was the first person he called upon release. I prayed for wisdom and prophesied to him. He would not spend a night in jail over this charge. He didn't.

...God uses people of all textures and dispositions.

Charges were reduced and eventually dropped. I was given the authority by the court system to oversee his menial community service. And, the relationship deepened. Mind you, I am still planting and watering. He is still a model father and being recommended for awards as such. Is he still rough around the edges? No. He is still rough all over. But, God uses people of all textures and dispositions. After all, didn't He use you and I?

Many Christians may have jumped down his throat at his response.

But, I had to laugh heartily in one of our conversations. I asked him to 'pray for me' in humor because I was going on vacation with three women; my wife, my daughter and her friend. His response tickled me. He said he would pray for me. His words were humorous but expressive in his unique manner. Many Christians may have jumped down his throat at his response.

Some people will come to God in an instant. Some will observe then come. Some will take a while.

He said, "I'm going to pray to Old Boy in Charge about you. It's rough being with a bunch of women. I know He will answer my prayer for you. I think He's hearing some of my prayers and helping me change. But, I know He knows who you are." I was in tears laughing when I got off the phone. The fallow ground was being broken up. We must allow those who are coming to God to be expressive in their own way until God through the Holy Spirit reveals to them otherwise. Some people will come to God in an instant. Some will observe then come. Some will take a while. And, He will harvest some along the way all the way up to their transition from the earth. God knows.

To just win the soul and not disciple them is the equivalent of giving someone a can of food but no opener.

I gave these examples because buzz words like "favor" are thrown out haphazardly. In the passage, there is no other option but favor being given by all the people. This is not limited to Christians in the church. Therefore, we must be wise to win souls. (I may step on toes here.) But, our mandate is to make disciples. You can't win souls by only going out during transportation to and from church. You can't make disciples by staying in the church.

To just win the soul and not disciple them is the equivalent of giving someone a can of food but no opener. You leave them to their own devices that may be disastrous. In order to win souls, you must go to them. In order to make disciples, you must bring them to Him. Selah…

8

LET GOD ADD TO THE CHURCH
(PROGRAMS VS PROCESS)

I have been guilty of speaking an untruthful statement concerning bringing people to the Lord. While I am now constantly aware of such a blunder, it still happens within the Body. The statement reflects a widespread sentiment. I hear the verbiage, "I got them saved". It is a lie. Only the Holy Spirit draws us in order for us to come to the Lord. If He doesn't draw us, we don't come; simple. Small slip ups like this very often open the door for confusion and total misunderstanding. The world watches every move we make.

Our evangelism should not be restricted to a planned event.

If I were to survey all Christians throughout the ages, I would almost be certain the vast majority did not initially hear the Gospel in a religious setting. They were busy in the marketplace, a social gathering, reading, or just listening to another's conversation. We have an unjust expectation to bring someone to "church" instead of being the meal on wheels for delivery. Our evangelism should not be restricted to a planned event.

As I am perusing the pericope of Scripture, I become continuously stuck on one phrase; "the Lord added to the church daily as such should be saved". This caught my eye and really made me think. Too often we have some type of assistance that we think we should use to present the Gospel; a hook of sorts. Well, I am not seeing that anywhere in the early church as recorded in the Book of Acts. All they did was continue in the apostle's doctrine of teaching with fellowship, praise God, go from house to house breaking bread and being in the temple on one accord. This brought the favor to them from all the people. This alone is what people were observing. And, the Lord, not programs, gimmicks and other activities, added to the church. It was Him, not them!

In this era, we tend to be activity oriented, attaching activity to every function which includes worship and fellowship. While it may be necessary and acceptable to many venues, is it so with the church? I truly don't think so. While the church is to be relevant to today's society, it is still to be a place of encounter with God; a place of reverence.

It is my own personal and humble belief that if we become the living epistles that Paul spoke of, we would be read by many more people than just those we encounter in church. I am thinking of an advertisement that I grew to show total disdain for.

When someone sees something continuously, whatever it is, they become familiar and gravitate to it.

I have resided most of my life on the eastern coast of America. Interstate 95 travels from Maine to Florida; a true north to south artery. It seems as if within a three state radius of the North Carolina and South Carolina border there are billboards inviting you to stop at 'South of the Border'. These billboards seemed to be every three feet in my mind (perhaps that is how fast I was driving). I didn't even want to stop at South of the Border. But, guess what? When I saw the exit, the car functioned with a mind apart from my mind! It pulled in, parked and the doors opened so I could go shop in overpriced stores with gouged gas prices!

Too often evangelism becomes a program instead of a lifestyle.

While I am being humorous, it is a point to be highlighted and made. When someone sees something continuously, whatever it is, they become familiar and gravitate to it. Could this be what we are missing in the Kingdom? How much are we showing what we need to in the Kingdom?

It was once jokingly stated that churches are responsible for the chicken almost going into extinction.

Too often evangelism becomes a program instead of a lifestyle. We are quick to create a function, activity or program designed to "draw" the people. Yet, I recall Christ saying if we lift Him up He will draw all men unto Himself. Let us begin to lift Him up instead of banners advertising fish dinners and barbeque platters. It was once jokingly stated that churches are responsible for the chicken almost going into extinction. I can't agree with it unless you include my mother in the equation. She once told me that if she didn't eat chicken at least once a day she didn't feel as if she had eaten. But, I think the point is made.

We are not called to all people in all things.

Programs and activities can never supersede the Word, prayer and fasting in evangelism. The community must be bathed in prayer and dwelled in by the Word; us as living epistles. There cannot be a separation of sorts. When I walk out of my house, so does my Bible. But, my Bible didn't get placed under my arm or proceeds out of my mouth in constant quoting. I must love everyone with the love of Christ. Do I fall short? Surely! But, I have the Holy Spirit that reminds me of me! And, I am constantly repenting, and adjusting daily. Let's face it. Some people are hard to love, beginning with the person glaring at you in the mirror. Yet, we make a conscious decision to do so.

We are not called to all people in all things. We have assigned individuals that we are to contact and connect with. While I may not be called to certain aspects of certain cultures, I am called to someone somewhere. This is where I function in my proverbial element. I am not called to someone that never experienced emotional or physical pain. But, if needed, the Lord will equip me instantaneously through the Holy Spirit to connect long enough to direct them to who can and will identify with them.

Christ began to move among those who were without.

When we remove the programs and activities while reaching to the root of the situation of salvation, we can begin the process. The process is just how Jesus began His ministry; going out from the synagogue, in our cases the churches. He didn't leave and never return. He just left out and began to touch those who were not in. Never did He negate the gathering of like-minded believers. He went to gather other like-minded people who wanted to be believers. It was just that simple.

We are worthless as lights if we are in a lantern convention.

Christ began to move among those who were without. Many possibly had a low self-esteem concerning their spiritual value for whatever reason. He came alongside them and walked with them. He interacted with love and teaching as He was in their presence. If you wish to win someone, you must be in close proximity to them. I do understand that many feel "those sinners" are in the dark and unreachable. But, "those saints" are supposed to be light to those in utter darkness. We are worthless as lights if we are in a lantern convention. Yet, even if we are but a penlight in darkness, the illumination we bring will be great! Get out of the pews and buildings and be love instead of just saying it.

The parables were so simple that many missed the true meanings.

Christ related the Kingdom of God to the people in relevant terms. He didn't use big words or lofty ideals. He used simplistic examples. The parables were so simple that many missed the true meanings. Yet, even in missing the meanings, they gained something. While they may not have received the wisdom of God, they received knowledge to give them insight in some matter of life. We must present the Gospel in such a pragmatic way as to assure the hearer that we are not so heavenly bound that we are no earthly good. When prompted, tell your whole unedited testimony not the edited churchified and sanitized one. Testify to those that are with you, not test-a-lie.

There are those times when your life and concern will speak more than a tent crusade with monstrous speakers and lights. I have been in communities where just my presence and concern is what led people to the Lord. I wasn't unapproachable or so "holy" that I couldn't be around others who were going through or stuck in something amiss. Why? I do remember my days of being "stuck" in something or being somewhere that I simply cried out to anyone that would hear. That One that heard was God speaking through an obedient and compassionate person.

I recall in one location, I was moving into an apartment building that housed elderly people. I had on old Army uniform pants with combat boots and a cut off shirt. Being an African-American male, I am very much aware of the stereotype given by media. As

I passed one elderly woman with empty hands she clutched her purse like a pit bull on a meaty bone. I never made any indication that I had seen her action or focused on it. I only wanted to move my belongings in so I could rest. As a matter of fact, I began speaking at every possible opportunity. I was most likely the youngest person in this very nice and historic apartment building. Most had been there for decades; being part of the semi-aristocratic group.

Eventually, I would receive greetings as they saw me leaving on Sundays and always reading something, whether a Bible, book or newspaper. I would strike up conversations attempting to get them to rent post office boxes or enroll in direct deposit for their retirement benefits. Many of the residents had their mailboxes broken into. Most eventually did rent mailboxes at the Post Office. One gentleman said he would never do it and was actually very rude to me at all times.

I am no way pacifist that thinks all Christians do not need to fight if necessary.

One day on the way home from work, I saw a man sneak up behind the grumpy old man who was checking his mailbox. I knew it was check day. He attacked him from behind and began to run up the street. Before he got fifty feet away I had tackled him and handled this coward. I am no way pacifist that thinks all Christians do not need to fight if necessary. Surely this was well in my earlier youthful years. I retrieved the mail and gave it to the man slightly perturbed since he never would even show gratitude. Yet, a seed was planted although I didn't think it would produce a harvest.

Not long after, I was approached by his female companion. Often elderly people may have companions of the opposite gender even if they don't wish to remarry after a spouse's transition. She wanted to be baptized and heard that I was a minister. She said that he told her he felt like a jerk because he treated the (Italian derogatory term for a Black man which I won't print) bad. And, I had helped him in his distress. After that he was very cordial to me, teaching me of a culture that I had only viewed in movies and in books. Wow. And, his companion was a staunch Southern Baptist woman raised in the Deep South in a place I had been stationed. This was beyond a stretch for her.

I had the opportunity to present the Gospel to them both in a way neither had ever heard. This was possibly the contractions prior to the birth of *The Community of We*.

He passed away suddenly. Yet, I did baptize his companion shortly afterwards. In NO way am I saying that baptism is required for salvation. She rededicated her life to the Lord and became quite an evangelist in the building.

She was such a lovely spirit. I would just enjoy her speaking of growing up in Georgia. She actually was born and raised in a town I had been stationed; proven to be an area of staunch segregation. There was such a difference in her description and mine for sure! Yet, here we were fellowshipping on a regular basis.

While living there in the period that had extended from one year to almost three, I had become somewhat of a building pastor. I performed pastoral duties even though there were members of various churches residing there.

These were mostly those who could not or would not attend a church.

I would be called on for many things. Comfort, alert, protection and guidance were all within a phone call or elevator ride. These were mostly those who could not or would not attend a church. Yet, the Lord added to the church daily as such should be saved. I hope the nugget in the previous sentence is understood. Function will create a filling of the church with those that the Lord is sending. But, first, we must function.

We are all familiar with certain aspects of culture and society.

Then there is a part of the process that calls for us to go against the grain. I call this the Samaritan visit. We are all familiar with certain aspects of culture and society. For some, it may take them to be in a hardship with another culture that was least expected to give aid. For others, God may call them completely out of their comfort zone for His purpose.

As for me, I have never been one that wished to remain inside the box. This is most likely what allowed me to survive and also caused much trouble in my youthful days. But, in retrospect it was all for His purpose and in the plan for my life.

In the military, if many went to the west, I would travel east. If they were part of the many, I sought out the few. If all joined one particular political party I had to at least research options often opting to remain independent. So, we all have to find that place of discomfort that will challenge our belief system.

I found it wonderfully interesting that in one of the parables concerning the man wounded on the road, the only person that stopped to help him was a Samaritan; that despised person to the Jews. Then in another account, Jesus "needed" to go through Samaria even though the Gospel was not yet to be preached outside of the Jews. He had a discourse with a woman at the well who was not a debutant in many eyes. Yet, it was imperative that the Lord stopped to speak with her in a discourse that primed the region for evangelism.

God called us to His purpose which is automatically uncomfortable to us.

I have ministered on this topic to various congregations and audiences. Each time the Lord gives a different 'spin' on this. The meat and potatoes are discomfort. But, the gravy is Gospel. Together, they are delicious! While the disciples were off on an errand (sometimes you have to send people away) the Lord was laying a foundation for later evangelism.

Again, we must realize that He never called us to comfort. God called us to His purpose which is automatically uncomfortable to us. Therefore we are to speak to those who we don't esteem to be familiar. How many blessings in the form of a different, unfamiliar person have we wrongly judged? The misconception is that the Samaritan woman was of ill repute. I beg to differ! I challenge those who wish to acknowledge and possibly correct an error in exegesis and eisegesis concerning this woman.

In the Hebrew culture it was not hard to divorce a woman. If she had "lost favor" in the eyes of the husband she could be divorced. Yet, in order to marry her, there must be a dowry that accompanied her to the union. If there was no dowry, then she could have been relegated to be a concubine. But, when the husband divorced her the dowry must be returned to her. Perhaps the fifth husband spent the dowry. Perhaps she was widowed five times. There are many possibilities that could have occurred.

Some well-meaning saint or preacher assigned her the title of a harlot, the same as they did Mary Magdalene. We should be very careful with our theological assumptions and stop repeating clichés that have been handed down generationally. We must continually go to the Word of God for our own revelation and illumination. Otherwise all we are doing is allowing the enemy to contaminate the Bread of Life that we receive.

Culture actually transcends race and religion.

I have been misjudged as well due to preconceived notions concerning culture which is not necessarily racial. Culture is nothing more in the Christian walk than the sum total of ways of living built up by a group of human beings and transmitted from one generation to another. Culture actually transcends race and religion.

Once we understand that we are to just flow in the direction and guidance of the Holy Spirit, then we can be change agents in our society. Once we master being the light instead of measuring lights, we will be the illuminating force that points people to the Christ. But, first we must grow up in Him that we may be more like Him; non-judgmental.

…there are times that come to my remembrance that I am glad He didn't draw me into the church.

That thought will always permeate my mind. The Lord is the one that will add everyone to the church as He has planned. To be honest, there are times that come to my remembrance that I am glad He didn't draw me into the church. No doubt, I needed to be saved. Yet, the Lord saw it fit for me to be preserved until the right moment. We do not determine that moment. Again, we do *NOT* determine that moment. It is He who determines the moment to draw us. We are the ones that must accept His invitation. I truly hope that we will grasp this concept fully and continue growing and going in Him.

9

DEHUMANIZATION OF A CULTURE IS NOT OF GOD

In recent years there is an increased dehumanization of individuals within specific cultures. This is not and never has been of God. To dehumanize someone or a group of people enables one to readily eradicate them from society. It is an action done often in military circles.

The culture of fear profits from the culture of fear.

In my own personal military service, dehumanization increased drastically at the hint of deployment to combat or upon arrival to a hostile zone. This enabled the soldier to engage and kill the enemy quicker than if he had to identify them as human. Even in American society, media has begun to clandestinely dehumanize individuals to enhance the culture of fear. The culture of fear profits from the culture of fear. But, do we believe media and society? Or do we believe God. I am of the inclination that when one wishes to dehumanize another, there is a deep seeded fear in their heart; low self-esteem with insecurity to be followed by blossoming hate.

It may not be for me or you to present the Gospel at specific times.

Are there individuals that operate in a subhuman fashion? Of course there are such individuals and even at times cultures. But, this does not negate the fact that they are still created in the image of God. In order to usher in the Kingdom of God, there must be a concerted effort to recognize every human being as His creation. I am fully aware that there are instances when an individual or groups operate at fully demonic levels. Yet, it does not negate the fact that they are human and deserving of the Gospel. It may not be for me or you to present the Gospel at specific times. But, God will ensure they have an opportunity to accept the Lord.

There are those that say if a mass murderer accepted the Lord his sin is not covered under the blood of Christ. Yes, it is. However, the consequences of his actions still prevail. This is the same as you and I. Unless in God chooses to miraculously erase all consequences (and my personal belief is that He will not violate His own principles of sowing and reaping) consequences will be part of the harvest. My prayer has personally been that the Lord would not allow me to reap a bountiful harvest from the wrong seed planted.

In the epistle to Titus, Paul addressed the dehumanization of the Cretans. He spoke stern about such things. Could that have been a civil rights issue of his day? There were many instances of racism, culture clashes, and segregation in the biblical accounts. Yet, Christ destroyed all of that upon Resurrection. We need to revisit that again totally.

It is imperative that we begin to walk in the reality of the Kingdom of God instead of societal norm to usher in "The Community of We".

Selah

10

CONCLUSION

I am truly humbled by God in being allowed to see myself in this work. The journey of this work has been one of many shifts in my spirit and conviction for actions not performed by me. Not only have I been required to confront the communal individual in the mirror. But, I have also had to confront beliefs and practices that are well meaning yet empty. I would be amiss to not mention the time in prayer and inquiring of the Lord how these words must impact me. There is no haphazard penning of thoughts without personal reflection often bringing about conviction primarily in the writer.

There are those in the Kingdom that are foundational, present and futuristic. Yet, all three dimensions of development are needed. God gives us communications whether through visions, dreams or just a quiet bombardment of our spirit. We must heed His communication which is full of direction. If we are led to places of unfamiliarity, then so be it. This is needed. Times like these are when the shift is not about us, but about our communities and embedding them with our existence and love. Somehow in our modern mindset we tend to write off the practices of the past as being obsolete. This is a grave error.

While I was not initially a church going person growing up, I did have some knowledge of this "God" that created everything. The household followed the norm for many in America; a Bible somewhere in the abode with a portrait, statue or medallion of Jesus. Christian holidays were celebrated but not necessarily in His honor. It was more of a societal adherence.

Then God began to speak to me. Surely, there was something of value to what my Aunt Betty was saying while she all but forced us to read from the Bible. She was the staunch Pentecostal in the family; the only one at the time. She was peculiar to most including me but consistent in her belief system. Other members of the family had beliefs and practices that appealed to my hunger for the knowledge of God. Some were sound. Yet, some were not sound at all.

Why fight something or Someone if there is no reality in the existence?

I am sure my neighbors were going to church every Sunday for a reason. But, they couldn't articulate it to me when I asked. It was like I had asked them for classified information! The answers that I received even in my own family were vague and sometimes hostile. I even deducted that those who peddled bean pies and a specific newspaper were inadvertently fueling my desire to know the God they said didn't exist. Why fight something or Someone if there is no reality in the existence? And, it all brought me to this writing; *"The Community of We"*.

All of these aspects of my own history blended to find the true God of the earth. Was He a segregationist? No. He has never been One to refuse anyone love. He designed us to go out into the world, not to come in and build walls.

While God did confuse our languages, it was to send us out to subdue the earth.

I found an interesting concept in the Book of Genesis. Often we are told that God punished man by confusing his language. This is not the case from my observation and reading of Genesis 11 and Genesis 12. We were to have dominion and subdue the earth as the initial mandate. Somehow under the leadership of Nimrod, mankind began to build a tower to go up instead of road to go out. While God did confuse our languages, it was to send us out to subdue the earth. This is the last instance of God coming down to earth to do something on His own.

In the very next chapter God chose Abram to work on His behalf in the earth. The mandate is given again; go out from what you see to the place that I will show you. This was the beginning of operating in a diverse community; evangelism. Abram, who was soon to become Abraham, became the father of many nations. The Hebrew people were dispersed to bring our God to others. And, many did convert to honor and serve Jehovah. God was sending His people out into the community, instead of keeping them sequestered with no contact.

Two nations are formed with the foundation of the God of Abraham, Isaac and Jacob. These countries are Israel and America. Israel was dispersed into the world thereby bringing their faith with them. Even in exile or under a conqueror their faith was noticed by the community. They were to present God to everyone with whom they interacted in some form or another.

Many are watching the lives and actions of all who name the name of Christ.

On the other hand America was founded on Judeo-Christian principles. And, we have everyone coming here walking into our beliefs as Disciples of Christ. At least they should see our faith in action when they come. I believe they will, and continue to do so until His imminent return. We have become that community of the collective "we" spoken of. We are diverse, yet functional. Many are watching the lives and actions of all who name the name of Christ. We have an unheralded opportunity to present Him to all.

Their names were changed in the spirit to be those who birthed many sons and daughters in the faith.

I have been blessed to return to a point of community impact from decades ago. Recently, I attended a banquet in honor of a couple who impacted a complete region with their faith and action. Like Abram, they left an area to travel to an area of direction. Once there they began to follow the precise instruction of the Lord in setting up His work. Their names were changed in the spirit to be those who birthed many sons and daughters in the faith.

Today many Christians would think tent revivals are outdated. I may beg to differ. While they may not be wise for all places and situations, they are in no way obsolete. We are earthen vessels carrying a treasure. We will not need the tent if we become garments of praise ready to cover those we meet.

I sat intently at the banquet and was almost in tears of joy listening to the rich history of the ministry. This was not a megachurch as heralded in this generation. Yet, it is a megachurch in the spirit to me. Swelling numbers do not impress me anymore. All growth is not good. Some growth is swelling. And, swelling can be a sign of infection. Not only were they impactful in the region, but also internationally. Yet, if you were to ride by their sanctuary, there would be no telltale sign of such power. It is just a humble location that is central to the city.

There are times when it is not about what you need, but the needs of those connected to you.

The founding apostle has gone to be with the Lord. His wonderful and faithful wife continues to head the ministry; continually walking in the vision that he began. The community that was touched by them extends through many countries and states, not just local communities. I saw at least five nations where their evangelism expanded and is still functional to this day. All they did was to be on one accord in the temple (the church); breaking bread from house to house, eating their food with gladness and singleness of heart (love), praising God and they had favor with all the people in the community. The Lord did the rest.

Being directed there by the Spirit of God, I am in awe. There are times when it is not about what you need, but the needs of those connected to you. In this case there are multiple connections that had to be made for a purpose of destiny. God will use specific situations and locations to get a person to a place for release such as with Abram. Such is the case of this ministry.

Others spoke of being fed, clothed and just given prayer as the church interacted with the community.

I listened intently as countless people spoke of how the founders would come into the community and begin to minister to the people of all cultures. One gentleman who was in the past a prominent disc jockey at one time is now a powerful minister of the Gospel. He shared how he would be in fear whenever he saw their tent being set up. His business must have decreased once the tent was erected. Others spoke of being fed, clothed and just given prayer as the church interacted with the community. The ministry didn't build a wall. They tore walls down to allow people to take refuge there. And, they did not have any program to get a person to accept the Lord as Savior except the Gospel, their life and their love for their neighbors.

It is my belief that we are returning to the basics of community. I anticipate that even though this ministry is now fifty years old, they are far from through. It is an example of success in community effectiveness. The founding apostle may be in the presence of God. His wife stated that she has more years behind her than in front of her. Yet, she is continually birthing sons and daughters into the Kingdom; equipping them to go out and form additional "communities" of faith and action.

We have examples given to us for all God has mandated us to accomplish. As stated earlier, Apostle Nate Holcomb said the church at its birth is the church at its best. My covering pastor has laid the foundation by teaching the church was built on prayer and the Word. This cannot be denied in any fashion. And, now in this lineage of ministry, I state that the Disciples of Christ must strive to return to the church at its birth. We must build the church of disciples by prayer and the Word of God and finally become "The Community of We", allowing God to have a place to add to the church daily.

In conclusion, I surely would be amiss if I didn't stand firmly on the concept of mercy. During the penning of this work, a friend of mine who, in the community of we, took gravely ill. He was rushed to the hospital with a grim prognosis. Yet, through the prayers of those on the faith side of the community, he did not transition. My personal prayer was that God would show him additional mercy because he was literally a jerk in accepting God's love. Even his wife had issues with him and the ridicule he would give. Yet, I didn't write him off and neither did she.

As I was praying for mercy and for him to have yet another chance to receive the Lord as Savior, God showed me something about myself. I was praying and saying how God had given so much mercy to this man. I actually thought that he had been given more mercy than me; silly me. The Lord showed me that we all have the same amount of mercy. God cannot divide mercy like a produce purchase. He is all-encompassing mercy alone in Himself.

While this incident was not his first time having to need emergency care and intervention, it is prayerfully his last. What the Lord showed me was that every time we need mercy we receive the full measure that is only found in Him. Mercy is only complete in the Lord. Therefore, God cannot section Himself off to be distributed in portions.

I had a few memories that came to my spirit and then my mind. Often there were flashes of things I either was directly involved in that the Lord didn't allow to kill me. Or, there were instances where I was redirected only to discover later of maladies that occurred. These were all example of mercy. And, even in these examples mercy was still at full effect. It only takes a smidgen of a millisecond to be killed or fall into injury.

I had to repent concerning how much mercy I felt was extended to him which I perceived was more than others. I received the same amount of mercy as the next person. We all receive the same amount through the sacrifice of Christ. He was sacrificed for sin. There was no measurement of big or little, many or few. It was sin; period. And, the Lord's mercies are new daily. He does not have a half mercy for today only to get a full mercy tomorrow. He is complete; Mercy Incarnate.

So, in this chastisement from the Lord, we are to extend the same mercy to the community; those without our fellowship. Too often we tend to misrepresent God and attempt to use His word to justify it; Galatians 6:10 specifically. How erroneous the church can be when establishing a wrongfully exclusive operation!!! Do good to all men; period. And, it is a shame that God used Paul to add, especially to those of the household of faith. Could it be that we don't show good to those in the household of faith? And, if we don't show this inside of the fellowship, how can we show this outside to the community?

We must live agape though Him. And, we certainly must show mercy at all costs understanding how He shows mercy continuously to us. After all, we are forgiven of our sin, but we still reap the harvest of the seed planted. Yet, mercy often prevents the full harvest of sin to come upon us. Let us keep in our mind the mercy we are continuously given knowing that it all began before the foundation of the world. Then we can dwell in *"The Community of We"*.

Selah

www.ingramcontent.com/pod-product-compliance
Lightning Source LLC
Chambersburg PA
CBHW050539300426
44113CB00012B/2188